SPACE TRAVEL AND EXPLORATION

Rebecca Clay

Series Editor:
Arthur Upgren, Professor of Astronomy
Wesleyan University

Twenty-First Century Books

A Division of Henry Holt and Company
New York

Twenty-First Century Books
A division of Henry Holt and Company, Inc.
115 West 18th Street
New York, New York 10011

Henry Holt® and colophon are registered trademarks of Henry Holt and Company, Inc.
Publishers since 1866

Published in Canada by Fitzhenry & Whiteside Ltd.
195 Allstate Parkway, Markham, Ontario L3R 4T8

Printed in the United States of America on acid free paper ∞.

Created and produced in association with Blackbirch Graphics, Inc.

Photo Credits

Cover (background) and pages 4, 11, 26: ©NASA; cover (inset) and pages 6, 18, 22, 25, 29, 32, 34, 35, 37, 44, 49: ©Photri, Inc.; p. 8: Library of Congress; pages 10, 53: AP/Wide World Photos; p. 17: ©Erik Viktor/Science Photo Library/Photo Researchers, Inc.; p. 38: NASA/Peter Arnold, Inc.; p. 42: ©Richard J. Wainscoat/Peter Arnold, Inc.; p. 46: ©David Parker/Science Photo Library/Photo Researchers, Inc.; p. 50: ©Mark Peterson/SABA; p. 56: ©Photofest; p. 58: ©Lucasfilm, Ltd./Photofest

Library of Congress Cataloging-in-Publication Data

Clay, Rebecca
    Space travel and exploration/Rebecca Clay
        p.   cm. — (Secrets of space)
    Includes bibliographical references and index.
    Summary: Describes the history and development of space stations and the exploration of our solar system, as well as the possibility of traveling to different stars.
    ISBN 0-8050-4474-4
    1. Astronauts—Juvenile literature. 2. Interplanetary voyages—Juvenile literature. 3. Outer space—Exploration—Juvenile literature. [1. Astronautics. 2. Interplanetary voyages. 3. Outer space—Exploration.]   I. Title. II. Series.
TL793.C627   1997
629.4—dc21   96-20070
                                                                                         CIP
                                                                                          AC

TABLE OF CONTENTS

INTRODUCTION

Humans have always been fascinated by space, but it has been only since the 1950s that technology has allowed us to actually travel beyond our Earth's atmosphere to explore the universe. What riches of knowledge this space exploration has brought us! All of the planets except Pluto have been mapped extensively, if not completely. Among the planets, only Pluto has not been visited by a space probe, and that will likely change soon. Men have walked on the Moon, and many of the satellites of Jupiter, Saturn, Uranus, and even Neptune have been investigated in detail.

We have learned the precise composition of the Sun and the atmospheres of the planets. We know more about comets, meteors, and asteroids than ever before. And many scientists now think there may be other forms of life in our galaxy and beyond.

In the *Secrets of Space* series, we journey through the wondrous world of space: our solar system, our galaxy, and our universe. It is a world seemingly without end, a world of endless fascination.

—Arthur Upgren
Professor of Astronomy
Wesleyan University

For many centuries, people dreamed of traveling toward the stars. In the 1960s, the first humans were launched into space. Apollo 11, shown here, carried the first astronauts to land on the Moon.

CHAPTER 1

THE GREAT ADVENTURE

The ancient Greek philosopher Aristotle once said that, "All men by nature desire knowledge." That desire has led to great explorations and discoveries in the history of humankind. Long before inventors found a way to lift a vehicle off Earth's surface and fly, people gazed up at the strange objects in the night sky and wondered what they were and how they might reach them.

In 1609, Italian astronomer Galileo Galilei was the first person to use a telescope to examine the sky above Earth. He could see that some of the "pinpoints of light in the night sky had mountains and moons." At the time, this was an amazing discovery because it meant that Earth was not the only planet in the universe. And if there were other planets, did that mean that there were other people or creatures out there? Today, we are still wondering the same thing.

In the eighteenth and nineteenth centuries, the Industrial Revolution produced new technologies that brought the dream of flying into space closer to reality. In 1903, the Wright brothers achieved the first powered airplane flights in history, setting the stage for the future of air travel. When rocket propulsion was discovered, it led to the firing of rockets in warfare. During World War II, the Germans created the V-2 liquid-fuel rocket. After the war, the U.S. Army began to test the V-2s for vertical flights, which can take off straight up from Earth, and to consider using them for flights into space someday.

Today, the space industry uses two kinds of rocket engines: solid-fuel rockets, which use chemicals that burn like gunpowder,

The success of the Wright brothers' airplane led to the invention of more powerful vehicles that would take humans higher into Earth's atmosphere, and beyond.

and liquid-fuel rockets, which have fuel tanks that drop away from the launched spacecraft once the fuel has been used.

Since the 1950s, the two most important participants in space travel have been the former Union of Soviet Socialist Republics (USSR, or the Soviet Union) and the United States. (In 1991, the Soviet Union was dissolved. Several republics split from Russia and became independent countries.) In the 1950s, the former USSR and the United States were both in search of knowledge and adventure. Because of their opposing political systems, however, they were also locked in intense competition with one another. This competition led each nation to spend huge amounts of money on developing their space programs. Their rivalry became known as the "space race" because each one wanted to be the first to reach the stars.

Today, Russia and the United States are working together to develop major space programs such as the *International Space Station*. Space agencies from Europe, Japan, Italy, and Canada, as well as private businesses, have also joined the effort. All those involved recognize the great potential for conducting experiments and manufacturing materials in outer space.

And They're Off!

The space age got off to an official start when the former USSR launched the world's first artificial satellite, the uncrewed *Sputnik 1*, in October 1957. A month later, it sent up *Sputnik 2* carrying a dog named Laika—the first living organism to travel in space. Unfortunately, the spacecraft was not designed to be recovered and Laika died in orbit. Today, Laika is remembered throughout

Yuri A. Gagarin was the first person to travel into outer space.

the world as the most famous Soviet cosmodog. There is even a rock 'n' roll band in Russia called *Laika and the Cosmonauts*.

The United States soon followed Russia by launching its first satellite, *Explorer 1*, in January 1958. That was also the year that the National Aeronautics and Space Administration (NASA) was created to plan and conduct all U.S. space activities, except those that were primarily military. Since then, Russia and the United States have launched thousands of spacecraft and 12 men have returned safely to Earth after walking on the surface of the Moon.

The Russians were the first to launch a man into space. On April 12, 1961, cosmonaut (the Russian term for astronaut) Yuri A. Gagarin made one orbit of Earth in *Vostok 1*, a tiny spaceship hardly big enough for one person. After 1 hour and 48 minutes in flight, he landed safely back in Russia. Gagarin was the first hero of the space age.

More "firsts" followed. On May 5, 1961, Alan B. Shepard, Jr., traveled in *Freedom 7* to become the first American in space. In 1962, John H. Glenn, Jr., became the first U.S. astronaut to orbit Earth. A year later, in 1963, the pilot of the *Vostok 6*—Russian cosmonaut Valentina Tereshkova—became the first woman in space. She orbited Earth 48 times. Twenty years later, in 1983, Sally Ride became the first American woman to make a spaceflight.

First to the Moon . . .

"The first step on the Moon was a step toward our sister planets and ultimately the stars. 'A small step for a man' was a statement of fact, 'a giant leap for mankind' is a hope for the future."
— Buzz Aldrin

Although the Russians were the first to launch a spaceship, Americans sent a man to the Moon before anyone else. *Apollo 11* carried astronauts Neil Armstrong, Edwin "Buzz" Aldrin, Jr., and Michael Collins to the Moon. On July 20, 1969, when Armstrong, dressed in his bulky space suit, placed a foot on lunar soil, people around the world witnessed the astonishing event on television. Fifteen minutes later, Aldrin joined

Edwin "Buzz" Aldrin, Jr., placed a U.S. flag on the surface of the Moon during *Apollo 11*'s historic visit there.

Neil Armstrong: First Man on the Moon

On July 16, 1969, three astronauts strapped them-selves into the *Apollo 11* spacecraft for a historic voyage to the Moon. Four days later, Neil Armstrong and Edwin "Buzz" Aldrin, Jr., landed the lunar module *Eagle* on the Moon while Michael Collins stayed behind on the *Apollo 11* command module, *Columbia*. A billion television viewers around the world erupted into cheers and tears as Neil Armstrong became the first human being to set foot on the Moon.

Born in Ohio in 1930, Neil Alden Armstrong earned his pilot's license be-fore he was old enough to drive a car. Later, he flew as a navy pilot during the Korean War. After graduating from

Purdue University in 1955, he joined the agency that would become known as NASA, then called the National Advisory Committee for Aero-nautics. He knew he wanted to be an astronaut, but he first flew as a research pilot for NASA. In 1962, Armstrong became the first civilian to enter the astronaut-training program.

Armstrong took his first trip into space in March 1966. He piloted the *Gemini 8* mission, during which two orbiting space-craft were physically joined together for the first time. A few years after his famous Moonwalk, he became professor of aero-space engineering at the University of Cincinnati. Today, he is married and has two sons.

Armstrong on the Moon's surface. Because there is only one sixth of Earth's gravity there, the astronauts bounced from place to place instead of being able to walk.

Today, nearly 30 years later, astronauts seem to have lost some of their interest in traveling to the Moon. With no water or air there, it seems like a dead world. In the future, however, the

Moon may be the setting for a lunar way-station that would make distant space travel easier. Scientists have suggested that the first habitat on the Moon might be inflatable. Then a small city might be built with houses and factories. Engineers could also mine the planet for materials to build spacecraft for missions to other planets, such as Mars. Launching these spacecraft from the Moon would save time, fuel, and money. Because of the Moon's clear atmosphere and its distance from Earth, astronomers have also suggested that an observatory be built there. High-powered telescopes used from the Moon could give us a closer look at the rest of the universe.

. . . Now on to Mars

Today, Mars—often called the Red Planet—is where the new generation of space travelers wants to go. This is especially true now that scientists have discovered a piece of the surface of Mars here on Earth that may contain the fossils of living organisms. This piece of Mars was found in the ice of Antarctica in 1996. Scientists theorize that the chunk was thrown off the Martian surface by an asteroid, and then flung onto Earth's surface. They wonder what other signs of life might be lurking within our neighboring planet. Some scientists want to take a crewed spacecraft there to find out.

We already know that Mars is more like Earth than any other planet in our solar system. Mars has weather, dust storms, its own moons, volcanoes, polar ice caps, and river valleys. Being farther away from the Sun than Earth, however, Mars is much colder. It has an extremely thin atmosphere and no ozone layer to protect life against the harsh ultraviolet radiation from the Sun. Dust storms can become so huge and dense that visitors to Mars would have to stay inside shelters for weeks at a time. How would human beings survive in such a world?

One method scientists propose is terraforming, a theoretical way to turn a lifeless globe like Mars into an Earthlike habitat with liquid water and living organisms. Science-fiction writer Jack Williamson used the term "terraforming" in a 1940s novel about engineers who bring a dead world to life.

The first step in terraforming Mars would be to warm the planet's atmosphere and melt its polar ice caps. This might be achieved by introducing dark algae that would grow on the frozen Martian surface and help raise the temperature. The algae—a simple plant form—would reproduce quickly and spread over the ice. Through photosynthesis, the algae would also create oxygen that would be discharged into the atmosphere. Over time, the ice caps would melt. Scientists also hope to blast through the planet's crust to release the carbon dioxide that they believe is hidden beneath it. This carbon dioxide might then be used for rocket fuel, making travel between Mars and Earth easier because spacecraft could be refueled upon reaching Mars. Although the Martian atmosphere is 95 percent carbon dioxide, there is not enough of it to make rocket fuel. The amount of carbon dioxide in Mars's thin atmosphere is quite small and considered unsuitable for fuel.

In the meantime, NASA has already begun a series of robotic missions to explore the possibilities of landing on Mars. The first spacecraft, or space rover, was launched in 1996 as part of the Mars Global Surveyor program. The rover was scheduled to map the planet's surface, to look at how minerals are distributed, and to monitor the weather there.

It was expected that it would take seven months for the small space rover to reach Mars, approaching the planet's orbit by aerobraking, a technique that helps save valuable fuel by using parachutes, rockets, and airbags to slow down the spacecraft. NASA plans five more robotic missions to Mars over the next decade, with the last one scheduled to take off in the year 2005.

What Then?

Researchers and engineers are continually developing new technologies that they hope will make space travel easier, safer, and more efficient. Most planets exert so much gravity on spaceships that they need tremendous amounts of fuel to liftoff and to land. Carrying these enormous fuel loads is not practical for today's spaceships. One of the biggest obstacles to distant space travel is developing propulsion engines that can operate without the heavy fuel now required for launches and landings.

Liquid-fuel propulsion engines cannot be used for traveling the vast distances from Earth to other planets, especially to those in different solar systems. At the relatively slow speeds most spacecraft travel today, it would take many lifetimes to reach other planets. Astronauts headed for a distant star would die long before their spaceship reached it.

For example, the nearest star to our solar system, Proxima Centauri, cannot be reached using present-day spacecraft. It is about 26 trillion miles (42 trillion kilometers) from Earth, or 4.3 light-years. Astronomers use light-years to measure huge distances in space. Light travels at about 186,000 miles (299,000 kilometers) per second. A light-year is the distance that a beam of light can travel in a year. A spaceship would have to fly at the speed of light, an impossible feat at this time, to get to Proxima Centauri from Earth in about four years and three months, or 4.3 light-years.

Looking for a faster way to travel through space, NASA has been working on a new kind of extremely fast spacecraft called the National Aero-Space Plane (NASP), or the X-30. The aerospaceplane would be especially valuable because it takes off and lands horizontally on a regular runway and flies directly into orbit. This system is called single stage to orbit (SSTO) because it does not require the huge solid-fuel rocket boosters

Sailing Through the Universe

One space exploration idea that scientists have been considering for several decades is the use of solar sails. Long before space scientists began to seriously design models for a solar sail, the science-fiction writer Arthur C. Clarke invented a solar-sail race from Earth to the Moon in his 1963 essay "The Wind from the Sun."

A solar sail is a vast but very thin sail, made of lightweight aluminized plastic. It uses the power of sunlight to move a spacecraft. Once launched by a rocket, a solar-sail spacecraft would coast without fuel or engines. A "space sailor" would adjust the position of the sail to slow down, to speed up, or to change the direction of the spacecraft.

A solar-sail spacecraft would travel much more slowly, but cover longer distances, than a rocket-propelled spacecraft. Its only propellant would be sunshine. A solar-sail spacecraft, for example, might take over a year to reach Mars while a rocket-propelled spacecraft would arrive in seven months. At first, solar-sail spacecraft could be launched to carry supplies to Mars ahead of a crewed expedition. With improved technology, solar sails might be able to propel ships carrying humans deeper into outer space.

The NASP, seen here in an artist's illustration, may one day replace the space shuttle as the primary vehicle for space travel.

that space shuttles now need. The NASP would look more like a supersonic airplane than a spaceship, and could be used to carry astronauts and supplies to an orbiting space station.

Because it would fly at very high speeds—up to several thousand miles per hour—the NASP would need a special engine, such as a ramjet. A ramjet uses hydrogen, a gas that exists throughout the universe, as fuel. A ramjet would be especially useful for flights beyond Earth's orbit since it could be refueled with the hydrogen found in space. An advanced version of the ramjet, the scramjet, uses a system that combines air and fuel. This mixture explodes and provides the thrust for the aerospaceplane to race through outer space.

In just 40 years, humans went from dreaming of space exploration to actually sending spaceships out to explore the universe. If so much could be done in such little time, imagine where we may be living and working in the next century. The sky is the limit!

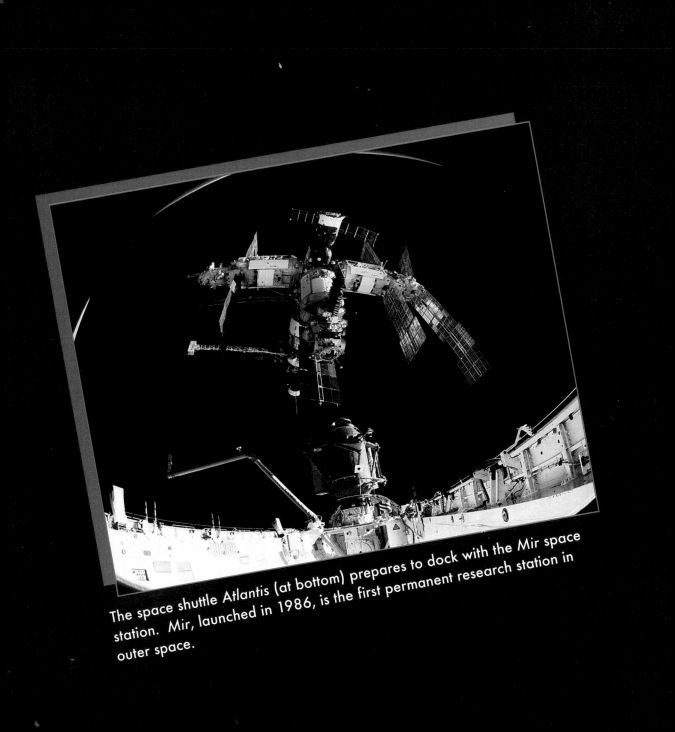

The space shuttle Atlantis (at bottom) prepares to dock with the Mir space station. Mir, launched in 1986, is the first permanent research station in outer space.

CHAPTER 2

"HOME AWAY FROM HOME"

The future of space travel and research will only be as exciting and successful as the astronauts and scientists of tomorrow can make it. The twentieth century has been a time of courageous experimentation, in which the world saw both amazing triumphs and tragic failures. In the twenty-first century, we must learn from our mistakes and take the next great leaps for humankind into outer space.

After the launching of short-term spaceships into orbit in the 1950s and 1960s, the American and Russian space agencies began developing permanent orbiting space stations where astronauts and scientists could live and work for extended periods of time. In 1971, Russia sent up the first of its *Salyut* space stations, in which cosmonauts could live for up to two months while orbiting Earth. A smaller craft called *Soyuz* carried up fresh supplies from Earth.

The *Salyut* provided the first opportunity for human beings to study the long-term physical effects of microgravity—also called zero gravity—such as weight loss and calcium depletion. When traveling in space, an astronaut experiences a feeling of weightlessness, similar to what you feel during the drop on a roller-coaster ride. Microgravity is the more accurate term because objects in space are still attracted to each other by gravity—only, not as strongly as they are on Earth.

Salyut became so popular that after a few years it was not big enough for the number of cosmonauts working in it. In 1973, Russia sent up a new *Salyut* that had room to store more supplies. This one became crowded, too, and soon an even bigger station was needed. *Salyut 7* was launched in 1977. It had two docking ports, allowing additional supply craft to land.

In 1986, the Russians launched the first *Mir* space station, which measured over 107 feet (33 meters) long and had 6 docking ports. Since then, *Mir*, which orbits Earth every 90 minutes, has been occupied almost continuously. Some cosmonauts have stayed on *Mir* for almost 400 days at a time. In 1995, as a sign of the growing cooperation between the Russian and American space agencies, Norman Thagard became the first U.S. astronaut to board the *Mir* space station. Russians and Americans have been working together on *Mir* ever since.

Laboratory in Space

In the 1960s, while designing its first space station, *Skylab*, NASA considered using a number of different shapes, including an inflatable donut and a wheel. The final design looked like a long cigar, or cylinder. In 1973, *Skylab* was launched on top of *Saturn V*, which was known as the rocket that never failed. Weighing about 85 tons (77 metric tons) and measuring 118 feet (36 meters) in length, the space station carried a three-man crew—Joseph Kerwin, Charles "Pete" Conrad, and Paul Weitz—for 28 days. Separated into two levels, *Skylab*'s upper floor contained space for storage and experiments. The lower floor was divided into the crew's living quarters, which included a dining room, bedrooms, and a bathroom.

Two more crews were launched during the next year, each setting a record for the length of time spent in space. The current American record was set by *Skylab III* at over 2,016 hours (84 days) and 1,214 orbits of Earth. The Skylab program totaled 513 man-days in orbit. Thousands of different experiments were conducted. In 1979, *Skylab* fell from orbit, more than five years after its last crew had returned home. Although most of the space station burned up in the atmosphere, a few pieces fell to Earth.

Skylab II, launched in July 1973, captured the attention of many high school science students around the country. NASA held a national contest for students to propose science experiments that could be conducted onboard the space station. From nearly 4,000 entries, 25 of the best were chosen. The students designed the experiments themselves.

For example, a Massachusetts student asked *Skylab II*'s three astronauts to bring along two common female spiders, named Arabella and Anita, to see how they would spin their webs in an environment with little gravity. When the astronauts first released the spiders into the orbiting spaceship, Arabella and Anita flopped around and bounced from wall to wall. The

The *Skylab* space station served as a working and living environment for U.S. astronauts. Here, astronauts onboard *Skylab II* conduct an experiment.

spiders, however, quickly adapted, and a few days later had spun the same kind of web they would have woven on Earth.

A Texas student asked the astronauts to test their hand-eye coordination by performing intricate moves while in orbit. Each astronaut had to insert a stylus (a thin instrument with a pointed head) into 119 small holes arranged in a maze. The experiment was a success—the astronauts' weightlessness did not affect their ability to do such precision work.

Students in Nebraska and California asked the astronauts to test how rice seeds would grow in microgravity. The astronauts planted the seeds while in orbit and found that they grew just as they would have on Earth. The seed experiment let space scientists know for the first time that it might be possible to grow plants during long space journeys, perhaps transporting them to distant planets as a food source.

Living in Space

A space station is designed to stay in orbit for years and provide a place for astronauts and scientists to live and work on a long-term basis. With almost no gravity onboard, its inhabitants float around its interior—mostly by pushing off one wall and coasting to the next.

Outer space is not a friendly environment for human beings and it presents many challenges that must be overcome. Space contains no air or oxygen, so humans need help to breathe. This means astronauts must wear specially designed space suits to protect themselves when working outside of a spacecraft. In addition, temperatures in outer space are extremely cold in the shade and deathly hot in direct sunlight. Solar radiation can be fatal to a person who is unprotected.

To prevent such problems, space travelers stay in their tightly sealed cabin—or wear space suits—where they breathe oxygen or purified air. Air conditioning controls the temperature and humidity inside the cabin and space suits. The exterior of the spacecraft is designed to reflect sunlight away from it, preventing solar radiation from destroying it. In the future, spacecraft on long interplanetary voyages might require heavy shielding to protect against intense exposure to solar radiation.

Reusable Rockets

A space shuttle is a rocket that is reusable, unlike most rockets that are fired once and then destroyed. In 1977, a passenger jumbo jet helped launch the first U.S. shuttle. It was called *Enterprise*, a name suggested by thousands of fans of the television series *Star Trek*. Since the early 1980s, space shuttles have been used to place satellites and telescopes into orbit, as well as to transport crew members and supplies to *Mir*.

A space shuttle has three major parts: the orbiter—which looks like an airplane—solid-fuel rocket boosters—of which there are two—and the external fuel tank used to launch the shuttle. Two minutes after takeoff, the boosters fall off the orbiter, and the fuel tank falls away about six minutes later.

Shuttles are launched vertically and return to Earth horizontally, unlike earlier spacecraft that splashed down into an ocean using parachutes to help slow their descent. Because it has no remaining fuel or power, a shuttle lands like a glider on a long runway. Future space shuttles will be designed to look like the aerospaceplane that was described in Chapter 1.

A shuttle's crew usually consists of two pilots and up to five mission specialists and/or payload specialists. Mission specialists work with the commander and pilot on such tasks as planning crew activities and running experiments. They may also work outside of the spacecraft and use remote manipulating systems. Payload specialists are responsible for deploying satellites and conducting experiments.

Shuttle launches were common in the 1980s, until the tragic explosion of the shuttle *Challenger* in 1986. The seven crew members of the twenty-fifth shuttle flight were instantly killed when a faulty sealant ring in a rocket booster failed. The shuttle blew apart when the leaky ring allowed liquid hydrogen and liquid oxygen fuels in the external tank to mix together and ignite. The *Challenger* disaster was a terrible blow to the nation and to the space program. New shuttle flights were delayed for over two years, and did not resume until the launch of the shuttle *Discovery* in September 1988.

International Space Station

During the 1980s, NASA developed plans for a huge space station called *Freedom*. However, the project seemed very expensive and some lawmakers wondered whether it should be abandoned. There were years of delay as the question was debated. Congress finally

The space shuttle *Atlantis* left its launch pad in Florida in a fiery takeoff in 1994. Over the years, NASA has had many successful space shuttle missions.

This computer-generated image of the *ISS* shows a space shuttle docked to it high above Earth.

voted to save the project and, in 1993, the White House asked NASA to redesign *Freedom* to make it less costly. Today, the project is called the *International Space Station (ISS)*, and is a smaller version of the original design. The *ISS* is being built with the cooperation of six space agencies from the United States, Russia, Europe, Japan, Canada, and Italy. These countries will build an international community and science institute in space.

If all goes as planned, it should take four-and-a-half years to build the *ISS* in space, piece by piece, starting in November 1997. That is when the United States and Russia will launch an uncrewed spacecraft into orbit as part of three construction phases. When completed, the space station will orbit Earth with a crew of six. It will be made mostly of special aluminum alloys (aluminum mixed with other metals) that are very tough and light. Some parts of the station will be almost as thin as the walls of a soda can, although they will be much stronger.

Because building the *ISS* will cost at least $26 billion, each of the six space agencies will be responsible for different phases during construction. For example, Russia, with 25 years of space station experience, will send up the first module containing living quarters for the crew members. The United States will send a laboratory module where science and technology experiments can be performed. Europe will contribute a research laboratory and a robot cargo ship. Japan will also send a research laboratory to be used to conduct experiments in the high vacuum and microgravity environment of space.

The Canadians will provide a 58-foot (18-meter) robot arm that can lift up to 220,000 pounds (100,000 kilograms) and move modules and other large elements of the space station. A smaller arm, about 12 feet (4 meters) long, will be used to replace small parts. Italy's modules will carry and store supplies such as food and scientific equipment.

The entire space station will get its power from two pairs of huge solar panels attached at each end. The solar panels will collect sunlight and turn it into electrical power to run experiments and life-support systems. Including the solar panels,

Shannon Lucid: 188 Days in Space

When Shannon Lucid landed on Earth in October 1996, after a record 188 days aboard the *Mir* space station, she had spent more time in space than any other American. After 140 days, Lucid became "stuck" in space when the first shuttle that was scheduled to bring her back was canceled due to safety problems. The next shuttle was canceled because of Hurricane Fran in September 1996.

Lucid's rescue team was expecting to have to carry her out of the space shuttle *Atlantis* on a stretcher. Most astronauts who spend such long periods of time in space cannot stand up on Earth right away because their bones have become too brittle from a loss of calcium. But the 53-year-old astronaut surprised everyone by walking out of the shuttle on her own.

The main reason Lucid was able to walk out of the shuttle was because she spent many hours working out on *Mir*'s exercise bicycle and treadmill. She wanted to prove that human beings could live and work in space for months at a time without serious health problems. To make her life onboard feel more like home, Lucid snacked on M&M's and bowls of pudding. Her daughters also sent her plenty to read. Delivered by supply shuttles, her favorite books were Charles Dickens's *David Copperfield* and anything about the American West.

Born in 1943, Lucid spent the first years of her life living with her family in China. Her sense of adventure has been strong ever since. She dreamed of being a pioneer and when she read a book about the rocket pioneer Robert Goddard, she decided to become a space explorer. Science was her favorite subject in school, and after graduating from high school she got her pilot's license.

After receiving her degree in chemistry from the University of Oklahoma, Lucid applied to NASA and was chosen to be one of the first six women to become astronauts, along with Sally Ride.

Shannon Lucid works with a Russian cosmonaut aboard Mir.

She took her first flight in 1985 aboard the space shuttle *Discovery.* Her mission to *Mir* was her fifth space flight. While onboard, she studied how a candle burns in space, how protein crystals grow, and how quail embryos—inside their eggshells—develop in microgravity.

After her return, Lucid was happy to be reunited with her husband and three grown children.

the completed space station will be 118 yards (108 meters) long and 81 yards (74 meters) wide—about the size of two football fields. Inside, there will be 43,000 cubic feet (1,204 cubic meters) of living and working space.

Three to six people will live on the station at any one time. Most will be scientists, but there will also be engineers, technicians, and management personnel. Each person will stay onboard the station for from three to five months. In general, it is not healthy to live in space much longer than that because weightlessness and the lack of gravity makes space pioneers lose muscle mass, as well as calcium and phosphorus from their bones. The loss occurs because the body changes without the pull of gravity. Fortunately, once astronauts return to Earth, they usually regain their normal muscle mass.

Once in microgravity, the slowing of calcium production in an astronaut's body begins almost immediately. This causes a person's bones to weaken. The longer a person remains in space, the more calcium he or she loses. Exercise can help prevent such problems, and astronauts will be able to ride an exercise bike while in orbit on the space station. The bike is like a regular exercise bike except that it has straps that hold the feet to the pedals and the body on the seat.

Experiments in Space

Based on past space experiments, scientists have discovered that low-gravity or microgravity conditions can be excellent for processing and manufacturing certain materials. They call this kind of work Materials Research and Processing in Space, or MRPS.

One experiment that astronauts will continue to conduct on-board the *International Space Station* involves the burning of a candle in microgravity. This experiment focuses on the process of combustion in space conditions. In normal gravity, a flame burns yellow and forms a vertical teardrop shape. In microgravity, however, since there is no "up" or "down," a flame burns a solid blue color in the shape of a sphere.

In addition, scientists will study how crystals grow in space. Many experiments with crystals have already been conducted on previous flights. If successful, specially grown crystals may be used to develop new drugs and to study diseases such as cancer and diabetes. Medical researchers also hope to take advantage of the low gravity in space laboratories to grow tissue to study arthritis and AIDS. They may also be able to grow proteins, which is part of the process of developing drugs.

Researchers will run experiments with electronics, biotechnology, metals and alloys, polymers and ceramics, and glass. In addition, they hope to make major improvements in semiconductors (materials that transfer or conduct electric current) and optical fibers. It may also be possible to create new products that have not yet been imagined by scientists on Earth.

The possibility of developing and manufacturing materials in space is of great interest to many parts of the business world. If such experiments are successful, private companies would help pay for shuttles and space stations to be built and launched in exchange for the opportunity to conduct their own research projects in space. Space travel is expensive, and combining resources from business and government could make it possible for many space dreams to come true.

The launch of the Russian satellite *Sputnik* began the space race between America and the former Soviet Union. Today, *Sputnik* is on display in a museum in Moscow.

CHAPTER 3

PROBING THE UNIVERSE

Before scientists were able to send the first human being into orbit, they began testing spacecraft that could carry equipment. They launched satellites to view Earth from hundreds of miles away, and space probes to investigate the Moon for a future landing. Today, although space agencies from different countries are most focused on building a huge space station or traveling to Mars, uncrewed spacecraft remain some of the most useful and important tools for exploring the universe.

Since *Sputnik* orbited Earth for the first time, thousands of astronomical satellites have been launched into space. (This does not include the many orbiting communications satellites used for transmitting phone calls and television signals, or weather satellites used to track and predict weather.)

This is an artist's conception of *IRAS* above Earth's atmosphere.

Satellites allow scientists to investigate the Sun, other stars, Earth, and outer space in general. Their position in orbit, away from Earth's dense atmosphere, allows them to collect better data than they could get from Earth's surface. Satellites are often outfitted with cameras, telescopes, radio receivers and transmitters, and other instruments.

The *Infrared Astronomical Satellite* (*IRAS*), a joint British-Dutch-American project launched in early 1983, probed the hidden reaches of our galaxy and was the first to discover disks of gas and dust around distant stars that might form new planets. An infrared satellite detects the faint heat from distant planets. The possibility of planets beyond our solar system is a great inspiration for space explorers who are eager to reach them someday.

The *IRAS* used liquid helium to keep its equipment cool. The liquid helium ran out in late 1983, and the satellite broke down.

Lunar Probes

With the hope of one day being the first to land a man on the Moon, both the former Soviet Union and the United States began sending lunar probes to investigate it. In 1959, the

Russian *Luna 2* was the first to reach the Moon before crashing into its surface 36 hours after launch. Later that year, *Luna 3* succeeded in going completely around the Moon, and it sent back the first photographs of the Moon's far side. And in 1964, the U.S. *Ranger 7* transmitted the first close-up pictures of the Moon before crashing into it.

In January 1966, the Russian *Luna 9* made the first soft landing of a spacecraft on the Moon—meaning that it landed without being destroyed. Later, Russian lunar probes scooped up soil and returned it to Earth to be analyzed. Some of the probes also deployed small roving vehicles to test lunar soil over a wide area. In May, five months after *Luna 9*, the United States followed with *Surveyor 1*, a lunar probe that sent back more than 11,000

The United States sent several *Surveyor* probes to explore the Moon. Here, technicians prepare *Surveyor 4* for a trip to the Moon in 1967.

close-up views of the Moon. Another U.S. probe, *Surveyor 3*, dug trenches on the Moon to study its surface properties.

The main objective of the American and Russian lunar probes was to explore the possibility of sending a man to the Moon. Photographs taken by the American probes were used to pick out a good landing site for the *Apollo 11* mission.

Space Probes

Beyond the Moon, spacecraft have landed on Mars and Venus, and have flown by Mercury, Jupiter, Saturn, Uranus, and Neptune. Space probes are useful in penetrating a planet's atmosphere and collecting information on its temperature, winds, soil, and chemical makeup. During the 1970s, both the United States and the former Soviet Union sent up space probes as often as possible.

Early attempts to land probes on Mars were unsuccessful. In 1971, the Russians were the first to send two probes to Mars. These probes, however, crash landed on the planet before they could transmit any significant data. Also in 1971, the U.S. *Mariner 9* orbited Mars and transmitted enough photographs back to Earth to allow scientists to create a map of the planet. The Russians tried again in 1973, but four more probes malfunctioned. At this time, they named two Martian craters after the science-fiction writers Jules Verne and H. G. Wells, a tribute to the inspiration these men gave to space explorers.

NASA launched *Pioneer 10* in 1972, and *Pioneer 11* in 1973. Traveling at 25,000 miles (40,000 kilometers) per hour, the two *Pioneers* were the fastest human-made objects at the time. They crossed the Moon's orbit in 11 hours, which was 6 times faster than any other spacecraft had ever done. Still tracked by scientists today, they are the first Earth-made objects to leave the known solar system.

Pioneer 10's first stop in 1972 was in Jupiter's system, 620 million miles (998 million kilometers) away, and it sent back the first close-up pictures of the planet and its moons. *Pioneer 11* sent back the first close-up photos of Saturn and its moons in 1973. *Pioneer 10* was the first spacecraft to pass safely through the unexplored Asteroid Belt and it was the first to send back pictures of Jupiter's Great Red Spot. Both *Pioneers* are now headed for the unknown reaches of the galaxy, studying the solar wind and cosmic rays entering our portion of the Milky Way.

In 1975, America's *Viking 1* and *Viking 2* were the first space vehicles to launch landers to the Martian surface, sending back the first close-up color photographs of the Red Planet. The *Vikings*

This model of the *Viking 2* lander shows the spacecraft on the surface of Mars.

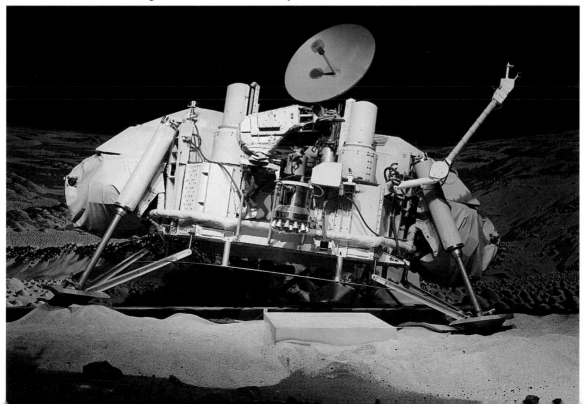

each traveled to Mars as a lander and orbiter joined together. The orbiters stayed in orbit while the landers actually touched down on the planet. Once there, they started studying the composition of the Martian soil and atmosphere.

The *Pioneers* paved the way for the next generation of spacecraft. In 1977, NASA launched two revolutionary space probes, *Voyager I* and *Voyager II*. Like the *Pioneers*, the *Voyagers* were sent out as observers, to explore the far reaches of our solar system and transmit information back to Earth. (Each *Voyager* is about the size of a small car and weighs about a ton.)

For power, the *Voyagers* use generators to convert plutonium (a radioactive element) into electricity. Their far-flung travels have helped us to understand our solar system, providing the first details of distant planets and their moons.

The *Voyagers'* main targets were Jupiter and Saturn. By using the force of gravity from each planet, they were able to essentially "fling" themselves to the next planet. This fuel-efficient

Voyager I sent photos of Saturn, such as this color-enhanced image, back to Earth.

The Sounds of Earth

Since the *Voyager* space probes will be traveling for many more years, toward worlds we can barely imagine, scientists decided that they should carry a message from the Earthlings that sent them.

Attached to each *Voyager* is a sort of time capsule, a gold-plated copper phonographic record with a cartridge and stylus and instructions for how to listen to it. The record's aluminum jacket is etched with scientific symbols that show where Earth is positioned in the galaxy. Sent in 1977, the record should last a billion years.

If extraterrestrial beings could figure out how to play the record, entitled *The Sounds of Earth*, they would learn about our human genes and how our brains work.

They could also listen to the music of Wolfgang Amadeus Mozart and Chuck Berry. The word "hello" is recorded in 60 different languages. All of the messages describe some aspect of what we know about our world and how we live. The song of the humpback whale is on the record as well. Scientists also included a complex recording of the sounds that the human brain, eyes, and muscles at work make.

If aliens find a *Voyager* vehicle, they will also find photographs of humans caring for one another, learning, and making tools and art.

system also allowed them to reach Uranus and Neptune. Both *Voyagers* should have enough plutonium power to keep sending back information through the year 2015.

It was important to design the *Voyagers* so that their antennae would point continually toward Earth, no matter where they went, and so that their cameras would move to face the objects being photographed. In 1980, when *Voyager I* flew by Saturn, about 885 million miles (1,424 million kilometers) away, it

Rocky the Rover

On July 4, 1997, a small, solar-powered, uncrewed spacecraft is scheduled to land on the planet Mars. Though it weighs just about 25 pounds (11 kilograms) and is only the size of a microwave oven, this little rover will carry enough computers, cameras, and other equipment to take important pictures of the Martian surface and analyze its rocks and soil. The rover's mission is to begin gathering information that could one day be used to land an astronaut on the Red Planet.

The new rover, called Rocky by its creators, is the first major step in NASA's Mars Global Surveyor program. By space industry standards, the cost of sending Rocky to Mars is cheap—about $260 million. Instead of using liquid fuel to land, Rocky will use air bags and parachutes to reach the planet's surface. Then it will bounce until it settles down.

The solar-powered rover will use a spectrometer (an instrument that splits a spectrum for study) to analyze bits of rock and soil, spending ten hours on each sample. Rocks often hold secrets to the history of a planet. From these rocks we might be able to determine if there was once life on Mars and if there ever might be life there in the future. Space scientists will be waiting eagerly to see what Rocky finds out.

sent images back to Earth that were remarkably clear and detailed. Scientists were thrilled to see how successful the probes had become. *Voyager II* photographed and measured the moons of Jupiter, including the moon named Titan.

Voyager II has traveled millions of miles to reach our solar system's more distant planets. In early 1986, *Voyager II* flew by Uranus—a blue planet—at about 35,000 miles (56,300 kilometers) per hour. The spacecraft transmitted photos that revealed that Uranus has 15 moons and is surrounded by pitch-black rings. In 1989, *Voyager II* arrived at Neptune and observed mysterious cloud patterns that looked like images seen through a kaleidoscope.

While the United States was focused on reaching Mars, the former Soviet Union was trying to get a spacecraft to Venus. In 1970, the Russians successfully landed the first probe on Venus, *Venera 7*, after three earlier probes were crushed like tin cans by the planet's high atmospheric pressure. To survive entry into Venus's atmosphere, *Venera 7* had to be heavily armored and reinforced, much like a modern submarine. In 1975, *Veneras 9 and 10* sent back the first black and white pictures of the planet's surface. The cameras revealed a barren landscape covered with rocks.

Later *Venera* spaceships carried radar telescopes. These telescopes transmitted images that revealed ridges and rings on Venus's surface. The rings may be the remains of old craters or volcanoes. Color photos returned to Earth showed that the skies of Venus are a yellow-orange, rather than the black skies previously seen from the surface of the Moon.

When designing their space probes, American scientists could not be sure that they would succeed in their mission to explore the outer reaches of our solar system. Imagine their surprise and excitement when the *Mariners*, *Vikings*, *Pioneers*, and *Voyagers* began sending back images of such astonishing beauty and detail that our knowledge of our neighboring planets grew by leaps and bounds. As these probes leave our solar system and travel toward distant stars, we will continue to examine the pictures they return to Earth, deepening our knowledge of the universe.

Modern observatories house powerful telescopes that allow us to see beyond our galaxy. In this time-lapsed image, star trails are visible above an observatory in Hawaii.

Before satellites and space stations, human beings watched the night sky through the lenses of telescopes. Invented in 1608 by a Dutch eyeglass maker named Hans Lippershey, the telescope was the first technology that allowed humans to see long distances. In 1609, Italian astronomer Galileo Galilei exhibited his version of the telescope and was the first to use it to scan the night sky. Galileo managed to observe the surface of the Moon. Today, modern telescopes can see billions of miles beyond our galaxy.

A telescope works by collecting light from a celestial object, bringing the light into focus, and producing a magnified image. The two most important types of optical telescopes are refractors, which use lenses, and reflectors, which use mirrors. Refractors were common in the nineteenth century and are rarely used today. The largest telescopes are reflecting, with two or more mirrors. One mirror collects the light from the object, while the other focuses the image.

The most famous of all telescopes today is the Hubble Space Telescope (HST), the first general-purpose orbiting observatory. Named after American astronomer Edwin P. Hubble, it was launched from the *Discovery* shuttle in April 1990. The telescope has five major scientific instruments. It has a wide-field planetary camera, faint object camera, faint object spectrograph, high-resolution spectrograph, and high-speed photometer. In 1997, the Hubble will get a new piece of equipment—an infrared camera that may be able to photograph evidence of other worlds.

NASA astronauts work to repair the Hubble.

The Hubble did not get off to a good start, and astronomers were afraid it would turn out to be a failure. First, a solar panel failed, and then, to their dismay, scientists discovered that the telescope's main mirror, almost 95 inches (241 centimeters) wide, was flawed. In December 1993, NASA sent a repair mission on the space shuttle *Endeavor* to fix the flawed mirror. The service mission was difficult and involved many complicated procedures. The shuttle crew had no way of knowing if the repairs had been accomplished.

The repair mission, however, *was* a success. Once fixed, Hubble began sending back some of the most astonishing photos of outer space ever seen. Their clarity was many times better than that of photographs taken through the most powerful telescopes on Earth. The HST has revealed the mysterious structures of distant galaxies. Hubble can also help scientists calculate how fast distant galaxies are moving away from our galaxy, the Milky Way. Such information can be used to help determine the age of the universe. The HST has provided the first convincing evidence of the existence of a black hole, which is a collapsed star that is so dense that light cannot escape its gravitational pull. The telescope also gave the world a clear view of what Jupiter looked like when pieces of the comet Shoemaker-Levy 9 slammed into the planet in July 1994.

Pictures beamed back to Earth by the HST have been so spectacular that they have inspired more people to think about the possibilities of space travel and what might be discovered by human beings exploring the universe. Hubble has seen planets in other solar systems—planets that revolve around stars like our Sun, and that may have atmospheres similar to our own.

Lenses and Mirrors

Today, the two largest reflecting telescopes in the world are the Keck telescopes at Mauna Kea Observatory in Hawaii. Keck I opened in 1991, and Keck II opened in 1994. Both have mirrors measuring 387 inches (983 centimeters) in diameter. Keck II also features an innovative design—instead of one piece of glass, its mirror is divided into 36 hexagonal segments aligned with one another. These segments make the telescope lighter and make polishing it easier.

One of the most amazing events astronomers were able to observe with the Keck telescopes was the comet Shoemaker-Levy 9 colliding with the planet Jupiter. They watched as pieces of the comet broke off and later hit the planet in different places. The telescopes photographed these points of impact and astronomers are still studying the pictures to learn much more about Jupiter. The Keck telescopes have also provided glimpses of very distant galaxies and the deepest reaches of the universe, including clouds of gas from the beginning of the universe.

The six mirrors on the MMT work together as one large mirror.

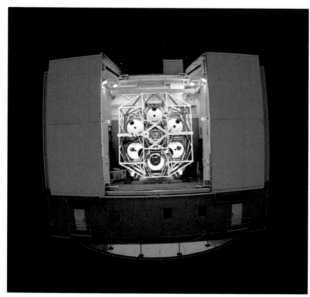

Another important telescope is the reflecting Multiple-Mirror Telescope (MMT), completed in 1979 on Mount Hopkins, south of Tucson, Arizona. The MMT is the fifth-largest reflecting telescope in the world. It uses a collection of six 72-inch (183-centimeter) mirrors working together to gather as much light as a single 176-inch (447-centimeter) reflector. As with the Keck telescopes, dividing a huge mirror into manageable segments is both desirable and necessary.

The portable Hopkins Ultraviolet Telescope (HUT) uses a spectrometer to study astronomical objects. In 1990 and 1995, HUT traveled onboard the space shuttle. One of the telescope's mirrors "spreads" the light from an object in space into a spectrum in much the same way that a prism breaks visible light into a rainbow of colors. The HUT then measures the brightness of the various colors and determines the object's composition and temperature. This allows HUT to observe wavelengths of light that are too short to be seen by the Hubble. The telescope was also able to study the cores of active galaxies, the relationship of two stars in a binary star system, and the characteristics of a nebula—a cloud of dust and gas.

Recently, a major new development for larger telescopes has been the addition of a charge-coupled device (CCD), which responds to light coming in from a celestial object by creating an image on a computer screen. This image can then be manipulated to improve the details, giving scientists clearer and closer views of such objects than they have ever had before.

Someday, astronomers at NASA would like to design and build a new generation of space telescopes that would be powerful enough to search for new worlds. Such telescopes might be able to locate and photograph Earthlike planets outside our solar system. The telescopes would have to be extremely powerful to pick up planets that are billions of times fainter than the star they revolve around—one telescope would have to have a mirror as wide as a football field is long. This is not yet possible with the technology that exists today. Instead, scientists would place several smaller telescopes far apart and combine their light to simulate one huge telescope.

Radio Telescopes

Instead of looking at light sources, radio telescopes listen for radio waves from space. Radio telescopes catch radio signals from space objects, including very active objects such as radio galaxies and quasars. A radio galaxy is a galaxy that emits extremely strong radio waves. A quasar is a quasi-stellar radio source, a kind of very small but powerful celestial object, similar to a galaxy. Radio telescopes have also recorded radio emissions from Jupiter.

The largest collection of radio telescopes in the world is the Very Large Array (VLA) near Socorro, New Mexico. A radio telescope consists of satellite-type dishes equipped with antennae that "listen" for radio signals from the universe. Built in 1980, the VLA features 27 antennae stretched across 13 miles (21 kilometers) in the shape of a Y. By combining the signals from all 27 of the dishes, the VLA can build an image of the sky that is more detailed than what one large antenna would receive.

Completed in 1993, the Very Long Baseline Array (VLBA) is a system of ten radio-telescope sites positioned across North America from Hawaii, to St. Croix in the U.S. Virgin Islands, to northeast Canada. The Very Large Array is also part of this system. These separate radio telescopes combine their images to work like one large telescope and produce sharper images than any other radio telescope.

In the future, astronomers hope to send a collection of satellite radio telescopes into orbit. They also would like to position radio telescopes on both Earth and the Moon that together would act like one enormous telescope 238,866 miles (384,400

This aerial view of the Very Large Array shows how the collection of its radio telescopes forms a Y.

kilometers) wide, the average distance between the two. As with the Very Long Baseline Array, images from the different telescopes would be combined to produce a more detailed picture of the universe.

By combining the stunning images from telescopes and space probes with the personal experiences astronauts have had onboard spaceships, human beings are quickly gaining enormous amounts of information about the universe in which we live. We have come a long way from the days when space travel and exploration were dreams imagined only in books of science fiction.

Science-fiction stories have entertained people for decades. Alien life-forms from these stories—such as the Borg seen here from the *Star Trek* series—inspire science-fiction fans to wonder "What if?"

CHAPTER 5

"IT'S A SCIENCE-FICTION WORLD"

Millions of children and adults throughout the world enjoy good science-fiction books, especially in America and Russia. High schools and colleges in the United States teach courses in science fiction, and hundreds of magazines are now available on the subject. Plus, every year thousands of fans attend special events like the World Science-Fiction Convention, and the World Science-Fiction Society Award ceremony where the best science-fiction creators are awarded "Hugo" statuettes shaped like rocket ships.

Since its beginning, science fiction has focused on themes such as traveling through space and time, bizarre life-forms on other planets, and crises created by alien creatures. Sometimes plots and descriptions are based on what is known about outer space at the time. Other story lines spring from writers' imaginations and have little to do with fact.

The term "science fiction" was first used in the 1920s by author and publisher Hugo Gernsback. He founded, and wrote for, the first science-fiction magazine—*Amazing Stories*. He called the new form of literature "scientification," but later changed it to science fiction to make it easier to pronounce. Gernsback thought that fiction would be a fun way to pass on scientific information and help create future scientists.

Science fiction began to be taken more seriously after two major events in the twentieth century: the explosion of the atomic bomb in 1945 and the successful Moon landing in 1969. Atomic energy and spaceflight had long been major subjects in science fiction, but they had been ridiculed as "mere science fiction." Soon, however, people could see that advances in science and technology were rapidly changing life as they knew it. This led science-fiction writer Isaac Asimov to say that we now live in a "science-fiction world."

Fact and Fiction

The first great creator of science fiction was the French writer, Jules Verne. One hundred and four years before the first manned landing, he imagined the future of space travel in the popular novel *From the Earth to the Moon* (1865). Later, he wrote *Round the Moon* (1870) and *Off on a Comet* (1877). Verne's facts were not always correct, and some of his situations were impossible, including one story where space travelers blasted off from a huge cannon in Florida.

A British citizen, H. G. Wells is often called the father of modern science fiction in the English language. Beginning in 1895, he wrote stories that were less scientifically based than those of Verne, but just as exciting. He published *The Time Machine, The First Men in the Moon, The Island of Dr. Moreau,* and the well-known *The War of the Worlds,* later made into a radio program and a motion picture.

Born in Russia in 1920, Isaac Asimov wrote more than 400 books based on both real science and science fiction. He sold his first stories to the new science-fiction magazine *Amazing Stories* in 1939. Asimov was a scientist himself, although his field was biochemistry, and not astronomy or any other space-related field. His best-known science-fiction books

H. G. Wells fascinated many readers with his science-fiction stories.

are *I, Robot* (1950), *The Foundation Trilogy* (1963), *The Gods Themselves* (1972), and *Foundation's Edge* (1982). Because of his extensive knowledge, Asimov also worked as a consultant for many "sci-fi" movies. He died in 1992.

As a child in Illinois, Ray Bradbury often suffered from terrible nightmares and frightening fantasies. When he grew older, he used his active imagination to write science-fiction novels and short stories. In 1941, he sold his first story at the age of 21, and became a full-time writer two years later. Bradbury's

Arthur C. Clarke: A Life Odyssey

Born in the seaside town of Minehead, Somerset, England, in 1917, Arthur C. Clarke was destined to become one of the most famous science-fiction authors of our time. Since his childhood, he was fascinated by science, and, after working in radar for the Royal Air Force, his first science-fiction story was published in 1946. He went on to write more than 60 books and to win the highest honors in the field of science fiction. He is perhaps best known for the 1968 screenplay he wrote with film director Stanley Kubrick: *2001: A Space Odyssey*, based on Clarke's own best-selling novel.

Clarke once said: "The only way of discovering the limits of the possible is to venture a little way past them into the impossible." Thus, he was not content with just writing fiction. In the 1940s, Clarke developed the first sketches of a satellite system that would relay radio and television signals all over the world. Many people were skeptical that such an invention would work. But 20 years later, the first communications satellites were launched into orbit. His invention would earn him honors from science institutes around the world.

In the 1950s, Clarke moved to Colombo, Sri Lanka, where he could combine two favorite activities—skin diving and photography. His love for the sea is similar to his love for outer space—both involve exploration and the feeling of weightlessness. Today, Arthur C. Clarke continues to write books and to communicate with his fans, from Sri Lanka.

best-known novel is *The Martian Chronicles* (1950), a story about Earth people who set up colonies on Mars.

The science-fiction novels and short stories of American writer Ursula K. Le Guin have captured the imagination of children and adults everywhere. The daughter of an anthropologist and a writer of children's books, Le Guin grew up immersed in legends and myths. Her many books include *Planet of Exile* (1966), *City of Illusions* (1967), and *The Left Hand of Darkness* (1969), which won a Hugo Award.

Just as they have been actively involved in developing a space program for years, the Russians have loved science fiction for many generations. One of their most popular writers is Konstantin Tsiolkovsky, who wrote about space exploration around the turn of the century. Tsiolkovsky was a scientist himself, and a pioneer in rocket and space research. His books include *Dreams of Earth and Sky* (1895), and *A Rocket into Cosmic Space* (1903), which describes a spaceship that uses liquid-fuel rockets. Russians have so loved and admired Tsiolkovsky that the Soviet space agency named a crater on the Moon's far side after him.

Space Creatures in the Living Room

Many children and adults in the 1930s and 1940s regularly listened to radio broadcasts of the science-fiction adventures of *Buck Rogers*. Since they could not see the action or characters described in the program, listeners had to use their imaginations to picture the strange worlds Buck visited and the unusual alien creatures he encountered as he traveled in outer space. Radio listeners also had to imagine him wearing his rocket-powered backpack and carrying his space gun as he rocketed from planet to planet, battling the deadly Catmen of Mars along the way.

In 1938, some listeners' imaginations were tricked by the radio program *The War of the Worlds*, based on the novel by H. G. Wells. Listeners who tuned in to the program after the introduction, when Orson Welles told listeners that it was fiction, panicked. They only heard that Martians had invaded New Jersey. Some people ran into the streets screaming with fright. It took several days for everyone to calm down and to realize that the broadcast was only radio actors playing make-believe.

When television arrived, producers also turned to science fiction for program ideas. In the 1950s, they broadcast shows like *Captain Video* and *Tom Corbett: Space Cadet*. Ten years later, viewers were watching *Lost in Space*, about the Robinson family, whose spaceship lands on the wrong planet, and *Star Trek*, about the *Starship Enterprise* and the adventures of its crew.

Star Trek became so popular that conventions still attract at least 10,000 "Trekkies" every year. Three other *Star Trek* series have appeared since the original premiered: *Star Trek: The Next Generation*, *Star Trek: Deep Space Nine*, and the most recent, *Star Trek: Voyager*. In all of these programs, characters must deal with extraterrestrial beings, some of whom are hostile and want to destroy the ship and its crew, and others who have valuable lessons to teach the human race.

The cast of *Star Trek: The Next Generation*. The series became famous for its portrayals of characters who traveled throughout the universe.

Science-fiction television in the 1990s also features programs in which aliens come to Earth, with both good and bad intentions. In *X-Files*, courageous investigators look into reports of bizarre events believed to be caused by extraterrestrial forces. And who says space creatures can't be funny? In the comedy *Third Rock from the Sun*, four aliens come to Earth to observe the behavior of human beings. The aliens pose as real people and find themselves acting strangely like humans.

Aliens and Popcorn

Writing about space aliens came first, and featuring them on radio was next. Then aliens began making appearances in movie theaters. Science fiction has fascinated movie makers since the early days of the film industry. The process of creating costumes, models, sets, and special effects to represent aliens and their worlds was exciting and challenging. In the beginning, most movies about space travel were adapted from science-fiction literature and from comic strips such as *Flash Gordon* and *Buck Rogers*.

The majority of science-fiction movies have been about alien beings, crazy scientists, and the evil aspects of technology. Many contained creatures so strange and frightening that they became known as horror or monster movies rather than science fiction. Sometimes the aliens traveled to Earth and created problems for human beings; other times astronauts found themselves on strange planets interacting with dangerous aliens. Many of these films reflected both the fascination and fear that Earthlings felt when thinking about outer space.

The earliest science-fiction movie was *A Trip to the Moon* made by French filmmaker and magician Georges Méliès in 1902. American inventor Thomas Edison's motion picture company produced *A Trip to Mars* in 1910. Science-fiction movies in the 1950s, such as *Destination Moon* and *The War of the Worlds*, won Academy Awards for their special effects.

In the 1960s and 1970s, science-fiction moviemaking became even more popular. Some of the best-known films from that era are *Fantastic Voyage* (1966), and *Planet of the Apes* (1968). In 1968, the movie *2001: A Space Odyssey* became one of the most widely discussed "sci-fi" motion pictures of all time. In 1977, *Star Wars* was one of the biggest movie box-office successes to date, and spawned several sequels. Beginning in 1979, the *Alien* movies, in which a parasitic monster lives

In a sequel to *Star Wars* called the *Empire Strikes Back*, the hero Luke Skywalker (right) meets with a wise life-form named Yoda.

on a spaceship and kills the astronauts, have kept millions of movie-goers on the edges of their seats. In the 1980s, the popular television series *Star Trek* was turned into several movies that used the same characters, and similar situations and themes. And in 1996, the movie *Independence Day*, in which humans successfully battle a major alien invasion, was a huge hit.

Coming Attractions

The courageous space travelers of the past 40 years, like the pioneers of the old West, have only recently opened the door to new and exciting worlds. So much has been learned from their willingness to risk their lives in pursuit of knowledge. And there is still an entire universe to explore and discover. In the twenty-first century, future generations of brave astronauts will go further and learn more than we can possibly imagine today.

Space scientists and engineers will gradually develop the technology to take them on voyages throughout our solar system and beyond. In just four decades, they went from developing the first rocket, to sending up a tiny, unmanned spaceship, to planning a huge space station with living and working quarters for a whole crew meant to stay in orbit for weeks at a time.

And who knows what tomorrow's space explorers will encounter: The space aliens of our science fiction, or life-forms that defy even our wildest imaginations? Will discoveries of unknown worlds help us create a better life on Earth? And what do we, as Earthlings, have to offer our neighbors in the universe? Such questions can only be answered when twenty-first century space pioneers explore the final frontier.

....

aerobraking A technique for slowing down a spaceship by using the resistance of the atmosphere.

astronomical satellite A satellite used only for astronomy research, such as observing our galaxy and the celestial bodies in it.

carbon dioxide A colorless gas that makes up less than one percent of Earth's atmosphere.

celestial Something that relates to the sky or visible universe.

combustion The act or instance of burning.

crystal A quartz that is most often transparent and colorless.

galaxy A large group of stars, dust, and gas held together by gravitational attraction.

generator A machine that generates electrical energy.

gravity The force of attraction that exists between two bodies.

lunar Relating to the Moon.

microgravity Having a small amount of gravity.

mission specialist A member of a spaceship crew responsible for planning crew activities, running experiments, and traveling outside the spacecraft, among other duties.

optical Relating to vision.

optical fibers Thin fibers of glass that transmit light.

ozone A gas that protects living organisms from harmful solar radiation that is also a serious air pollutant.

payload specialist A member of a spaceship crew responsible for deploying satellites and conducting experiments, among other duties.

photometer An instrument that measures the luminous intensity, or brightness, of an object.

plutonium A radioactive element.

polymers Chemical compounds.

propulsion A force that propels, or drives an object forward.

quasar An extremely bright celestial object that is similar to a galaxy.

satellite A celestial or human-made object that orbits another large body, such as a planet; the Moon is Earth's natural satellite.

spectrograph An instrument that can photograph the spectrum.

spectrometer An instrument that splits a spectrum for study.

spectrum A picture showing the intensity of electromagnetic radiation at different wavelengths throughout a given range, after radiation from a given source has been passed through a prism. The visible band of colors range from red to violet.

terraforming To change a planet's lifeless surface into a habitat in which living organisms can survive.

vacuum A space that contains no matter.

FURTHER READING

Berliner, Don. *Our Future in Space.* Minneapolis, MN: Lerner Publications Company, 1991.

Burns, Khephra and William Miles. *Black Stars in Orbit: NASA's African-American Astronauts.* Orlando, FL: Harcourt Brace & Company, 1995.

Cole, Michael D. *Apollo 11: First Moon Landing.* Springfield, New Jersey: Enslow Publishers, 1995.

De Somma, Vince. *The Mission to Mars and Beyond.* New York: Chelsea House, 1992.

Ride, Sally. *To Space and Back.* New York: Lothrop, Lee & Shepard, 1989.

Sagan, Carl. *Cosmos.* New York: Random House, 1995.

_____. *Pale Blue Dot: A Vision of the Human Future in Space.* New York: Random House, 1994.

Starbound (Voyage Through the Universe). Alexandria, VA: Time-Life Books, 1991.

ON-LINE

NASA's Office of Space Flight has a website that provides information about worldwide spaceflight missions. This website can be found at http://titania.osf.hq.nasa.gov/Welcome.html

To learn "everything you want to know about Mars," visit NASA's Center for Mars Exploration. It has current news, previous mission information, and much more. It can be found at http://cmex-www.arc.nasa.gov/

NASA's Information on Becoming an Astronaut page links to all sorts of space-related information from around the world. It can be found at http://titania.osf.hq.nasa.gov/hotlist/#astronaut

The Space News home page is a news weekly for the international space community. It offers current news, interviews, and compelling images that can be downloaded. Visit it at http://www.spacenews.com

The Aero and SPACE website was created in 1992. It explores career possibilities within the aerospace industry in a comic book format. This site was designed for middle schoolers to educate them about the industry. Visit it at http://graphix2.larc.nasa.gov/gs/samples/multi/022/022_00.html

Live from the Hubble Space Telescope is a site that allows visitors to interact with leading astronomers as they make observations using the Hubble. It can be found at http://quest.arc.nasa.gov/hst/about/easy.html

The Space Camp site offers visitors information about the U.S. Space Camp programs for children of all ages who dream of becoming astronauts. It also has Quick Time Virtual Reality movies and interesting images. Visit it at http://www.spacecamp.com

SOURCES

Barbree, Jay. *A Journey Through Time: Exploring the Universe with the Hubble Space Telescope.* New York: Viking Studio Books, 1995.
Begley, Sharon. "Down to Earth." *Newsweek,* October 7, 1996.
———. "Mission to Mars." *Newsweek,* September 23, 1996.

Chartrand, Mark. *Exploring Space: A Guide to Exploration of the Universe*. Racine, WI: Golden Books, 1991.

Dowling, Claudia Glenn. "The Mission Continues." *Life*, February 1996.

Jaroff, Leon. "Life on Mars." *Time*, August 19, 1996.

Jastrow, Robert. *Journey to the Stars*. New York: Bantam Books, 1989.

Lemonick, Michael D. "Searching for Other Worlds." *Time*, February 5, 1996.

Morrow, Lance. "Listening for Aliens." *Time*, February 5, 1996.

Murray, Bruce C. *Journey Into Space: The First Three Decades of Space Exploration*. New York: Norton, 1989.

Neal, Valerie, editor. *Where Next, Columbus?* New York: Oxford University Press, 1994.

Rogers, Adam. "Jupiter Steals the Show." *Newsweek*, August 26, 1996.

Royte, Elizabeth. "America Steps Boldly Back into Space." *Life*, February 1996.

INDEX